Table of Contents

Yes, It *CAN* Happen to You!

If you think you are too smart to get caught up in an Internet-based scam, well, I would suggest that you not bet on it. I certainly felt that way – until yesterday afternoon. Yep, scammed, jammed, rammed, and not even a "thank you, 'mam". I will break it down for you on a play-by-play basis, then give you some resources I was given during my FBI visit, and finally explain the subsequent actions of the site where I encountered the opportunity to be swindled. Those sections will contain all the facts that are either in evidence or can readily be produced. Then, as closing remarks, I will try to point the way to prevent a recurrence of any such events, certainly for me, and hopefully the networking site through which a lot of us are connected.

But, before I head into that, let me tell you how utterly embarrassed and ashamed I am of taking the bait. I _know_ I'm smarter than that. Damn, I have a PhD in Leadership Studies with research and writings in Business Ethics as a specialty of interest. I'm certainly not bragging about that last part. On the one hand, I am trying to tell you that these guys are very, very good. On the other hand, I am also going to tell you to what extent I have exercised my responsibility to abide by my own set of rules. But, I figured if I stayed completely quiet, there might be other victims, with the exception of my closest friends, and that would not be living up to my own standards. So, I plan to lay it all out, the good, the bad, the ugly, the thought process, the logic that drove some of the decisions, and I would venture a dangerous assumption that it could happen to you much easier than you might like to think. My intent is to inform you and make you think!

Hopefully you will be enlightened, or, if you have been the unwitting victim of a similar scam and said nothing it will help you come out to expose all we can about these operatives. Believe me, I understand. Due to the overwhelming feeling of stupidity the first reaction was to just stay quiet and hope none of your closest friends will find out. I'm here to tell you, my conscious and my education both told me that would be exactly the wrong thing to do and even something the perpetrators are banking on…literally! If you question what I am saying, think of the personal violation encountered by rape. We all know that staying quiet promotes more similar crime by the same individual. Well, this is absolutely no different. If we are to clean it up, we have to get it out there, so, that is what I am doing.

The Play-by-Play

The site offered an "Online Job Offer" posting. It was completely innocent and benign received from a very trusted source...the site. It was not your standard Craigslist or Facebook with completely open enrollment and the only monitor was other people posting a negative response after the fact and usually after considerable damage had been done. The site is by invitation only. The User Agreement for the site and constant reminders indicated you should not invite nor accept an invitation from anyone you do not know.

I took that commitment very seriously. At one point, I even had a request from a business associate for a work reference to be posted to the site. Before I agreed to do that, I did some due diligence on the person's background as it was posted on the site. Well, it seems that I was unable to verify some of the claims and when asked directly the member declined to provide any confirmation (even became quite insulted that I would even question it). As a result I did not post a recommendation. Like I said, I take the commitment to integrity very seriously, whether from a simple electronic "I Agree" by checking the box, or a more formal written contract. In my view they were both the same.

A major intent of this writing is to elicit the same feeling of commitment in you - the reader. Without this level of recognition that we are all connected on these types of social or professional networking sites and we must police our own at the gate, eventually the solution will fail and many of us will have to find the next alternative. Let me offer a quick example and then I will provide the facts of my particular incident.

During a homeowners' meeting one member of the 75-80 home neighborhood association was particularly outspoken about increased security patrols. The impact of the cost, by the way, was to be borne equally by all 75-80 of us. The reason for his adamant, consistent request was the occurrence of several robberies at his residence. There had been no other such incidents anywhere else in the neighborhood. I immediately suggested he check his guest list for the parties the couple was fond of hosting. That's what I am saying in this paper – check the guest before you invite them to the party, please.

This specific job offer was to provide services for the employer at a pay rate of $45.00 per hour with a requirement of 3-5 hours per day to conduct the company's business. The required activities in the job descriptions were itemized as follows:

- "Maintain up-to-date billing system
- Follow up, collection and allocation of payments
- Preparing, receiving of Payments.
- Carry out billing, collection and reporting activities according to specific deadlines
- Reconciliation of accounts
- Follow established procedures for processing receipts, cash etc
- Prepare bank deposits
- Print and mail out checks
- Process adjustments
- Organizing a recovery system and initiate collection efforts
- Taking surveys of check cashing stores and Western union".

Sure, I can do that, I thought. Sure, you can do that, you would think. Then the offer followed with:

- "Competitive Pay
- Paid Vacation & Holidays
- Career Advancement Opportunities

- You will be paid $45 per hour and there are compensations during holidays".

Well, who wouldn't be interested if you had been unemployed or under-employed for several months in the current economy? Or, you were in need of some extra cash to meet increased or unexpected expenses. It included the ability to work from home, use the Internet, control your own schedule, required no specific dress code and numerous other personal incentives. Sure, you would take the first piece of bait to check it out. You know, the old "nothing ventured, nothing gained" mentality. Besides, there was no request for up-front money, no request for personal information such as banking, no social security or credit card numbers to be provided, nothing to risk by learning more details from an application...right? And the application was simply the submission of a resume' to see if you were qualified.

So, place yourself in that position (and you will surely be there unexpectedly) and ask yourself, why not? Now, answer honestly, I think you would have sent them a resume'. You've already provided it to anybody willing to talk about an opportunity anyway as you look for work. Besides, you were responding to an advertisement posted on a respected, by invitation only, member only site that you had used successfully over the past several years. Well, if you can't put yourself in such a semi-desperate position, you probably won't agree with much of the following. But, before you close the book on this one, I would caution you, as I'm certain you have heard - "never say never" and keep reading. I'm telling you, it *can* happen to you!

The next piece of the job offer looked like the following:

"Hello,

Your resume is under review so fill this form and send it back ASAP:

- First Name:
- Last Name:
- Country:
- State:
- City:
- Zip code:
- Phone #:
- Have you ever been convicted for any crime?:

Send me your mailing address and your assignment will be given to you".

Well, again, certainly nothing sensitive in this request. The mailing address is a requirement to do the work and complete the forms described in the job description. So, why not? Done. Remember, the concerns were still present. That nagging thought of being scammed. But, so far, pretty innocuous information had been requested and nothing more than any company would ask for when hiring you...right? Right. Besides, the referral was from a trusted, members-only, by invitation site anyway.

To confirm your understanding you emailed back for clarification and receive the following:

"You will be receiving a petty cash payment, this will serve the purpose of your first assignment. Instructions will be given you on how to carry out this assignment, as soon as you get the package notify me by email. Reply to confirm receipt of email and proper understanding of contents".

In addition, just to be on the safe side, as you were always suspicious, you had not given them your primary address anyway. Let's say you gave them the address of your second home or your weekend place to keep it out of the mainstream of your life just in case something really was amiss with the operation it would be much easier to isolate. This meant that any mail arriving addressed to you would have to be from someone <u>very</u> select that had been intentionally given this particular address. So, you confirmed and waited for the mail to arrive with your "petty cash" and first assignment.

You put it out of your mind, sort of. A couple of days went by and nothing in the mail box. The weekend passed, nothing in the mail box. The following week, about mid-week, a plain white envelope arrived with no return address and a mailing label addressed to you. Under more normal circumstances at your primary address it would immediately go unopened into the trash. But, it was addressed to you and the only piece of mail in over a year that was sent to you at this address. It had to be the petty cash, an assignment, and the opportunity to start making $700 - $800 per week. You opened the envelope expecting a couple of hundred dollars at the most to start the process.

You were right. Well, at least partially. There was a check in the envelope. But, by your standards it was beyond petty cash. The check, from an unknown company in Los Angeles, was for slightly over $2,500.00 and there was no assignment included. Wow, that was suspicious. All the anxiety over being scammed erupts again. You researched the company from Los Angeles on the Internet and found it to be legitimate. Anyway, you have their check and they have none of your personal information, so, where was the scam? Just wait. Keep reading.

You did the prudent thing and let it sit for the day. After all, it came via regular mail, so they had no way of knowing when it arrived. You tried to think it through. Where was the scam? Nope, still no scam. You then contact the company by email to notify them you had received what you assume to be their "petty cash" check and you question that. Their response was the following request:

> "Yes. Deposit the check into your bank account and then with cash in hand proceed to the nearest Western Union location closest to you and have money sent to our agent in WA. Here are the details:
>
> (Omitted for security reasons)
>
> This is an urgent assignment, which needs to be carried out ASAP. Get back to me with details of money sent."

Aha, the scam! They wanted you to send money from your account that would be covered later by this bogus check. So, you told yourself, "I'm smarter than that and it was not going to happen". You fire off an email telling them that you will not wire any money from the deposit until their check has cleared your bank. You even tell them that if the assignment is so "urgent" they should find someone else to represent them. The emailed response from them is "OK, they will wait for the funds to clear" and to simply notify them when the check had cleared. Well, that was not at all what you expected. But, it did calm the anxiety and reversed your opinion that you had found the scam. So, what was the scam became an almost constant thought.

Over the next couple of days you checked your bank account on the Internet and the deposit was still pending, as it should be. On the third day, the amount was deposited into your account. With that, you contacted your bank by phone to verify the funds available as shown on your Internet banking site. You were told, "yes the funds were there, but only as a courtesy to you as a customer and if you questioned the validity of the deposit you should wait 8-10 business days to make absolutely certain it had cleared".

Here was the thought process and the exact email conversation that took place. Remember, the job offer was from a <u>trusted</u> source. It was not received through an unsolicited email. It was not garnered from Craigslist. It was from a members-only, by invitation only, site that you have rightfully trusted for business transactions and relationships in the past and not been disappointed. Having said that, to make sure you know what was going through my mind and what could likely be going through yours under similar circumstances, read the following emailed conversation:

> **ME:** "My bank has made the funds available, but, recommended that I wait 10 business days to make sure the deposit is not returned. My problem with the leap of faith is that it would hurt if I had to cover the amount. So, do I trust that it is legit or not?
>
> The reason I am having trouble is a lack of understanding of the business model and absence of any documentation you referenced in your solicitation, e.g. tracking on receivables, collections, record keeping, etc. So, either help me out in understanding or we wait another 9 business days making it 4/28 before I transfer funds out at your direction. Nothing personal, I hope you understand. Just experienced and not all good."

THEM: "It's good to read from you, as I have been expecting a message from you. Yes I have gotten a message also from my account officer that money has already been deducted from the account.
Now that funds are available you are to complete your first assignment which is sending money through western union to our shipping agent in WA. Here are his details again:

(Omitted for security reasons)

Immediately he has gotten this he will notify me after pick up and your next assignment will be given you.
As regards the funds being returned, nothing of that nature will be encountered because my account officer is handling all funds going in and out of this account and he is receiving instructions directly from me.
The urgency of the assignment should be understood and attended to.
My shipping agent has been expecting funds from you which will be used in purchasing some office supplies and other materials needed for your job and this will

be done as soon as he receives the cash today.

All business proceeds from the onset has been legit and I believe I am dealing with someone legit which is you. I can assure you that you are having no problems as far as your employment and financial issues are concerned.

Get back to me with details as soon as you have sent money."

For some strange reason, not the least of which was your trust in the source of the job opportunity, you proceeded to conduct the transaction as requested and ignored the statement of the clerk at your bank. You notified your new employer of the Western Union transaction information that you have wired $2,200.00, plus a $175.00 fee using their money. You then received the following email:

THEM: "I have received all details from you and i have forwarded this to my agent and finance officer. Again tomorrow you will be receiving instructions on your next assignment and I want the finishing process to be sped up. You did a great job with this but I believe you can do better. I will also like the following details to be provided:

1) Customer Reception
2) Time taken
3) Smartness of attendant.

Please get back to me with these details."

Being the diligent person that you are, you awaited the next assignment and kept track of your time to forecast your first paycheck. The next time the assignment arrived via FedEx. Not really an assignment, only a check in a plain white envelope inside the FedEx Letter envelope and from the same company in Los Angeles. For some reason, perhaps it was the recommendation from the clerk at the bank that you decided not to heed, you did not immediately notify the company of its arrival, but proceeded across town to present the new check to their bank for cash. This one was in the amount of slightly over $5,300.00 and you were not about to try and cover that if there was a scam going on.

Here's the biggie – the bank teller at their bank, while looking at his computer screen you assumed to verify the funds availability in the account proceeded to routinely ask you a couple of questions about your desire to cash a check of that amount like - Where did you get it? Did you know the people that issued it? Did you know what the company did that provided it to you? Was the check for some product or services that you had provided. Apparently convinced after your responses that you were not involved in the scam informed you that the check was a **fraud**! Get that, a **fraudulent check.** Not Insufficient Funds, but a ***fraudulent check***! That sinks it. <u>You've been scammed!</u> Son-of-a-bitch! Now what?

Well, first things first, go face what was probably not going to be good news at your bank. You drove back across town, in a bit of a daze, certainly angry, mostly at yourself (if you are being honest with yourself), and you found the message you were by now expecting...you learned the first check had been denied by their bank as a ***fraudulent check***. Get that? You are now out $2,375.00 that was the value of the Western Union wire transfer you trustingly sent last week. I don't know about you, but, to most of us that is still a lot of money to lose for simple stupidity. At this point I would interject...please, let the stupidity be mine and not yours.

Now what? Read on, even if you are much smarter than I am and will never get involved in such a scam, you will want to know what happens. Here's why I said that – as we get smarter, so do the crooks!

Resources & Recovery

The banker suggested that I go to the local police and file a report. I told them the check had been sent to me using the U.S. Postal Service from California and I had transferred the money using Western Union to the state of Washington, so I felt I should report it to the FBI due to the aspect of the check was mailed across state lines and now we had possibly had a wire fraud involved. She agreed. I looked up the location of the local branch of the FBI, as it was not someplace with which I was familiar (thank goodness), and drove directly to their office.

The authorities at the FBI office were very hospitable and sympathetic, but, in reality felt they could be of no assistance, and here is why...I went into the office to report "check fraud" and that was the wrong terminology. As I was quickly informed by the agent, I was actually reporting an Internet scam of which I was the victim. In addition, the amount of the scam was well below their threshold for getting involved.

He explained that I really had no idea where in the world the actual location of these people was as they were no doubt using fake information all the way around. The actual operations center was probably somewhere half a world away. I showed him the return address on the FedEx I had received, but, as he rightly pointed out, that meant nothing and it certainly did not mean that was the origination point of the scam. He expressed the fact that the scam was most likely being run from a country in Africa, say Nigeria, where cooperation for any prosecution with United States Federal authorities was not exactly high on their priority list. Thieves in other parts of world are not treated very harshly for stealing from an American by their local authorities. As an example, consider the recent outbreak of piracy off the coast of Somalia. Rampant lawlessness certainly does exist outside our immediate world, but, it can find a hospitable environment and greatly extend its reach with Internet access and a few unwitting suckers like me, or you.

Don't get me wrong, the agent had a very good understanding of my situation and I believe would have provided any assistance possible. Bottom line, there was just nothing he could do. The crooks are certainly smart enough to keep it well under the radar of our law enforcement. So remember $2,375.00 (US) will go a long way in a third world country. However, you would have to add a couple of zeros on the end to get the resources of the FBI involved.

He suggested I visit the following three websites and in this order:

1. www.ic3.gov – This is the FBI's official Internet Crime Complaint Center website. It allows you to file your complaint with the hope that the FBI will be able to match it to some pattern or larger situation. I logged on and filed a complaint as soon as I got back to my home base. Unfortunately, as with most law enforcement of this nature, it is a reactive, after-the-fact situation and they are certainly not in the business of making restitution. Nor should they be.

2. www.lookstoogoodtobetrue.com - Man, did the name of this website ring a huge bell in my head. This website is about fraud prevention and has numerous links that would have been helpful in advance. To quote directly from the home page because I certainly could not have said it any better...

    "Every day, American consumers receive offers that just sound too good to be true. In the past, these offers came through the mail or by telephone. Now the con artists and swindlers have found a new avenue to pitch their frauds — the Internet. The on-line scams know no national borders or boundaries; they respect no investigative jurisdictions. But, as with all scammers, they have one objective — to separate you from your money!

An interesting point about fraud is that it is a crime in which you decide on whether to participate. Hanging up the phone or not responding to shady mailings or emails makes it difficult for the scammer to commit fraud. But con artists are very persuasive, using all types of excuses, explanations, and offers to lead you — and your money — away from common sense.

This website was developed to arm you with information so you don't fall victim to these Internet scam artists. Education, good judgment, and a healthy dose of skepticism are the best defenses against becoming a victim. Remember, if it looks too good to be true, it probably is!"

3. www.ftc.gov – Yep, you guessed it, the Federal Trade Commission. After my visit, I could certainly understand why the agent placed this one last on the list. No doubt what would be needed is all in there, but, it is not an easy site to navigate and not at all focused on Internet fraud of consumers as are the first two listings.

I am sure there are numerous other sites and some are better than others. I have provided these certainly not as any form of a compendium on the subject, just to let you know what I was given as a list of possible resources by the local FBI field office.

As you can surmise, the net result of my morning was totally negative. I spent no time trying to place blame. It was obviously squarely on my shoulders. Also squarely on my shoulders was replenishing the $2,375.00 that had now been stolen from my account. That meant it was time to begin recovery. There was certainly no time to lose. As I approached the end of this little story and booklet on the subject, understand that all of this had occurred within 24 hours of finding out I had been scammed – and that included this writing.

I guess one thing I had learned along the way, the faster you can "get over it" (whatever "it" happens to be) and put a plan of action in place, the faster you can start to heal the wound that has been caused by "it". With that, my thoughts turned to making sure it did not happen to someone else, at least not within my broadcast range. I had to think, what did that mean? To me, it meant going back to the source of the first introduction – my trusted site of member only, invitation only connections.

Wow, that meant bearing my stupidity to my closest friends and business associates. That meant pushing an admission through my network, including Twitter that said "Hello friends and neighbors, I'm an idiot and I have just been swindled". What kind of a message was that for all to see? Not a very good one in my opinion, or so I thought at first. However, the more I dwelled on the concept, the more I realized that I was completely mistaken. Actually, it was exactly the opposite. I owed my friends and business associates the story to make them aware.

We're not talking about an awareness gleaned by seeing a one minute news blurb on television, or reading an article in a newspaper, or getting an alert posted through a website, or even an email from a trusted friend that I could forward on to others. We're talking about first-hand knowledge. Been there, done that knowledge. Remember the example I gave in the opening about the violation of rape. Well, in the final analysis, if I don't cry out and report the fraud then I am simply contributing to the perpetrator's ability to continue to commit it...right? Let me answer that for you...right!

    That train of thought led me to a resolution...write a paper that told the story. That would have some value. Post the events on a blog. That might help get the word out. Then the thought expanded to this little booklet you are reading. That would have even greater value. I could tell the story, weave in some assistance, provide the stated resolution of the hosting site (next section) and maybe it would have a more lasting value and far greater reach. So, please, if you have followed me this far, let's complete the journey with the site's resolution and some closing remarks.

Site Provider Actions

I will admit, at first it was difficult getting through to a live person and that simply added to my frustration with all the other events of the day. Their automated attendant on the phone indicated I should do everything through their website. This is the same website that had introduced me to the opportunity to conduct a fraudulent business transaction. After all, the Internet is their stock in trade. There is no retail outlet equipped to have live, real time interaction with the customer. It is simply not part of their business model. I even had to go outside the website to get a phone number for the company. I did feel this was a very unique circumstance. However, at this point, I was left no choice but to follow their process and hope for the best.

I completed a Customer Service Request as instructed, was assigned a ticket number by the automated web attendant, and was left with a very empty feeling when the email arrived giving me the ticket number and the guarantee of a response in the next 24 hours. Well, as you can imagine, I was in no shape to wait that long for the first response. I kept calling the company until I was finally able to

get a real human on the other end of the phone –
the operator.

I explained the situation to her. I made it
very clear my primary concern was the integrity and
reputation of their site. The entire foundation of
their business model is built on trust among the
members. As I stated early on, the rules for
participation were well articulated and stringent,
particularly by social or business networking
standards, and that was exactly why I liked the site
and trusted the connection that had now stolen my
money. I was not looking for restitution, I was
looking for satisfaction that I had been instrumental
in eliminating the threat to other members of a
worldwide network in the millions of people.

I simply stated that the site had been
compromised and was hosting the recruiting
process of a confirmed check fraud operation. Once
I got that point across she was responsive and
transferred me directly into Customer Service. The
phone was answered by the same voice mail
message to complete a Customer Service Request
form on the website and submit it. Trust me, that
didn't sit well. I did leave the message that I had
already done that, gave them the number of the
ticket as emailed to me by the automated process,
and expressed my concern that this was really not a

situation that allowed for the usual process to be completed and find resolution. Fraud was being perpetrated through their site and it needed to be stopped sooner rather than later.

That message must have resonated. I did get a return phone call within 10-15 minutes from an attentive, live operator in Customer Service. As I explained the situation to her and the sequence of events, she must have signaled her supervisor to read what she was typing as we conversed. The supervisor intervened and requested that I email an outline of the story you have just read, as it was briefly told to the customer service representative, directly to her email address. In addition, she requested that I also forward all my correspondence with the perpetrators. I, of course, quickly and gladly complied with both requests.

Very quickly after that I received the following email from the company:

"Hello Richard,

We have located the profiles that the postings have been made under and are taking the appropriate actions, starting with the removal of the jobs. Thank you for bringing this to our attention and our sincere apologies for any inconvenience you have experienced."

To be honest, it was considerably more than an "inconvenience", but I understood where she was coming from and made nothing of it. The main thing to be expressed here is the prompt, direct, and assertive manner in which the situation was handled. It has already gone a long way to restore my trust in the site. It was really never the site's "fault" as we would all agree. It was mine. But, there is an unwritten understanding and / or assumption that everyone on the site had read the rules and was abiding by them. But, unfortunately for me, apparently not.

Closing Remarks

A lack of trust can greatly lessen the value of any service being provided. Our mutual service provider totally understood that this – the trust of the members – was one of their primary assets and even a strategic advantage as they build their network. So, it is up to us to help make them successful and in turn it will make us successful.

I close my 24 hour ordeal with an admonition to "police" your area. I know we all want to grow. It's the "American Way". But, this is one environment in which we have to exercise some control of our growth. We must all only include other trusted sources. If you question anything about an individual in your group or your personal network, please, for the protection of us all (and that would include you) take the time and effort to do your due diligence. It will always be less of an effort up front than it is to clean up after a breach. It is the networking implementation of an auditor's statement – "trust but verify".

Hopefully you have found my little story helpful. Hopefully it will raise your awareness and prevent you from suffering the same consequences.

If you purchased this booklet, I thank you for helping me get the word out. If it was given to you by a friend, thank the friend. Please, continue to trust, conduct verification when you feel it is warranted, and we can all get back to the basics of building whatever it is that interests us by connecting with friends, business associates and growing our network of like minded professionals.

The world must be built on trust. Actually, I failed that miserably or you would not have been reading this. I failed to trust my banking clerk, because I *wanted* to trust my networking website. I failed to trust my instinct, because I *wanted* to make some money, easy money, too easy. I failed to trust my roots and my certain knowledge that "if it looks too good to be true, it probably is" as the second of the FBI recommended websites is titled.

So, please, learn from my mistakes. Don't make your own on this particular matter. The Internet is a wonderful, yet dangerous place that not only provides us the opportunity to reach places that are far away, it also allows those places to reach us and it can be someone you certainly would not knowingly invite into your home.

Thank you,

Richard Mays Owen, PMP, PhD

richardmaysowen@gmail.com
or
http://www.linkedin.com/in/richardmaysowen
or
http://www.twitter.com/doctorethics